"I'm new at this process an invaluable... Organized, easy to rea information. I'll use it as I learn system. Highly recommended!"

— Roger Ragan, Amazon Reviewer

"If you are new at the Kindle publishing game or even if you aren't, this book has a lot of very well thought out, intensely researched and intelligent information. The book is broken down into sections that are easy to understand and even includes links that any author can utilize to make their publishing/selling experience a more productive one."

— Ionia Martin, Top 500 Amazon Reviewer

"Corson-Knowles has developed a system whereby he has been able to earn a full-time income by self-publishing ebooks on amazon... in just eight months. He gives details in how he does it, a procedure that readers can copy. The book is written in simple language, is easy to follow, and it contains examples. People who want to sell ebooks will benefit from this author's advice."

— Israel Draznin, Top 1000 Reviewer, Vine Voice

"I have on my computer over 30 different programs and books about writing and selling Kindle books. Tom's book **The Kindle Publishing Bible** is one of the best. His advice is solid, easy to implement and very practical. Great information on choosing a title and some excellent resources to help you get the best title possible... If you want to sell more books, **The Kindle Publishing Bible** is a must have."

— J. Testerman, Amazon Reviewer

THE KINDLE PUBLISHING BIBLE

HOW TO SELL MORE KINDLE EBOOKS ON AMAZON

TOM CORSON-KNOWLES

Get the free Kindle publishing and marketing video training series here:

EbookPublishingSchool.com

TABLE OF CONTENTS

WHY I WROTE THIS BOOK

I'm an author just like you...

I self-publish my books on Amazon Kindle and I now earn a full-time income as a self-published author just 8 months after publishing my first book on Kindle.

But the truth is I had an upper hand, an "unfair advantage" if you will...

You see, I'm a member of an elite Kindle publishing authors society and I have been trained by some of the best Kindle authors, publishers and online marketers in the world.

But the training wasn't what I expected. Soon after I joined this elite society (referred to as The Society from here on), I realized that the world of Kindle publishing is filled with deception, lies and manipulation. Many so-called authors just hire someone in the Phillippines or India to write books for them, publish them under a pen name and then use all kinds of shady and unethical "marketing" tactics to sell more books.

Many authors even create fake accounts and leave themselves biased, glowing 5-star reviews. Others take it one step further - they'll even create fake accounts and leave YOUR book a 1 or 2-star review so that you can never compete with them. But that was just the tip of the iceberg in the world of selling Kindle ebooks and I was just getting started in The Society...

Since then, I've realized that the deception, lies and manipulation in the industry aren't just isolated events. It's part of the system... part of a system passed down from the old days of traditional publishing, simply being emulated in the online environment without the resources and financial backing traditionally published authors used to have.

In this book I'm going to share with you the truth about what goes on in the ebook industry. I'm not going to hold back or sugarcoat it like some other "best-selling" Kindle authors out there. I'm not going to tell you to do unethical things like create fake accounts and maliciously leave negative reviews for your competitors.

I'm not going to give you fluff either – just the real (ethical) action steps you need to take to sell more ebooks on Kindle starting today. I won't give you a single piece of advice without giving you the action steps to take and the information as to why it will help you sell more books.

The truth is I want to show you how you can sell more books in an ethical way.

Why? Because I believe authors like you and me – people with an important message to share – are able to change the world. Our words can bring readers from darkness into light. From sadness to joy. From grief to gratitude. From pain to pleasure. From boredom to enjoyment. From listlessness to purpose. From poverty to wealth. From weakness to strength. From ignorance to education.

I believe you have an important message to share. That's why you're reading this book. I want to help you get your message out there. And make more money doing it.

Are you ready? Let's go!

WHY YOU SHOULD READ THIS BOOK

There's a war out there in Kindle publishing. It's "every author for himself" (or herself) – at least that's how most of your competitors look at it.

But I've found that it just doesn't pay to do things unethically. Sure, there are many unethical ways to sell more books. But at the end of the day is that really what writing books is about?

I don't think so!

I write books to help, inspire and educate people. I write books to make a difference. And I hope you do too.

If your mission is to help inspire, educate and entertain the world, this book will give you the free marketing tools and strategies you need to sell more books fast.

This book will help you sell more Kindle ebooks – I guarantee it!

Chapter 1. How To Choose Your Best-Selling Book Title

Choosing the title of your book is probably the most important decision you will make when it comes to selling more Kindle books. Your book title alone will be responsible for a large percentage of your sales – so choose wisely!

Best-selling authors and publishers have known for hundreds of years that the title of the book will do more to increase sales than any other single decision you make about your book. Luckily for us, someone already did the research!

What Makes a Great Book Title?

Whether you're a non-fiction writer or a novelist or anything in between, a good book title is as necessary as a good newspaper headline. Without a good title, no one is going to open the book in the first place (or click on the link for ebooks)!

For example, would you rather read: "Think and Grow Rich" or "Contemplate and Increase Your Wealth Gradually Over Time as You Become a More Successful Person."

You probably know that the first book has been a best-seller for almost a hundred years whereas the second one has such a horrible title that it's likely no one would ever read it even if the content of the book was the same as Think and Grow Rich!

But why is the first title a "good title" and the second one not?

It's all about what the customer wants! But what does the customer really want in a book title?

HALDEMAN-JULIUS' BOOK TITLE TESTING

Emanuel Haldeman-Julius was an American author, editor and publisher in the early 1900s and he sold more than 200 million books in about 20 years. He had a unique way of testing his book marketing – he would change the titles of his books and see which titles sold better. In fact, Haldeman-Julius would take his books that didn't sell well to "The Hospital" where he would change their name and republish them in hopes of attracting more sales.

So if you've already published a book with miserable sales figures, maybe it's time to take it to The Hospital!

Here are some examples of name changes from The Hospital that dramatically improved book sales:

Los Precieuses Ridicules sold nearly zero books a year. When changed to *Ridiculous Women*, it sold over 10,000 copies a year.

Gautier's Fleece of Gold sold 6,000 a year. When changed to *The Quest for a Blonde Mistress*, over 50,000 were sold annually.

Le Bourgeois Gentilhomme when changed to *The Show Off*, took sales from slightly above zero to 10,000 annually.

The Mystery of the Iron Mask sold a respectable 11,000 a year but when changed to *The Mystery of the Man in the Iron Mask*, over 30,000 were sold that year.

5

The King Enjoys Himself sold 8,000 but *The Lustful King Enjoys Himself* sold 38,000.

None Beneath the King sold 6,000 while *None Beneath the King Shall Enjoy This Woman* sold 34,000.

Ten O'clock sold 2,000 but *What Art Should Mean To You* sold 9,000.

Art of Controversy sold zero while *How To Argue Logically* sold 30,000.

Casanova and His Loves sold 8,000 but *Casanova, History's Greatest Lover* sold more than 22,000.

Apothegems sold 2,000 while *Terse Truths About the Riddle of Life* sold 9,000.

Will o' the Mill and Markheim (both in one volume) sold almost zero copies but *Markheim's Murder* sold 7,000.

Pen, Pencil and Poison sold 5,000 while *The Story of a Notorious Criminal* sold 15,800.

Haldeman-Julius drew a few conclusions from his book titles that I think all authors should know and understand today:

USE DESCRIPTIVE TITLES, NOT POETIC TITLES

Pen, Pencil and Poison is a good example of this – it's purely a poetic title and its sales were miserable. *The Story of a Notorious Criminal* is much more descriptive and the reader actually knows what the story is about before she opens the book. Your customer must have a basic understanding of what the book is about or they will not buy it!

Use Simple Language, Not Esoteric Words

Not sure what esoteric means? Then don't use it in your book title! Avoid words that only a few people might understand. Instead, use simple words and clear language so that even the most humble readers can understand and relate to your book.

Even if you're writing a book on rocket science, you can sell a lot more books by writing in plain English for curious readers like me. And if you're not writing a book on rocket science, what's your excuse for using big words no one can understand?

If a Book Doesn't Sell, Change The Title

Haldeman-Julius and his incredible publishing career has proven, beyond a doubt, that a book title is crucial to making sales. If a book has distribution and marketing but is still not selling well, then the title should be changed thoughtfully to increase sales.

In this book, I'm going to teach you how to get the distribution and marketing. And if you try all the marketing strategies we'll be discussing and your book still doesn't sell well, then don't be afraid to change your title! I think you will be delighted with the results.

Now let's talk about a few other important ideas you should consider when choosing a best-selling title for your book.

WIIFM

You've probably heard the acronym WIIFM before – it stands for "What's In It For Me?" and it's the question every person asks when looking at a book and reading a book title. If the book title doesn't immediately answer the question or at least give you a visual image of an answer, you are likely to move on.

At the core, each of us are lazy in our thinking when it comes to buying something. We would much rather read a book title and instantly decide to read it or not than spend a few precious seconds or even minutes wondering what it's actually about. If your book title confuses your customer they won't buy!

"The confused mind always says no" is an apt saying.

Think and Grow Rich immediately tells the reader "I'm going to help you get rich!" and the reader believes it instantly – only based on the title of the book! The book could contain absolutely useless information but the title alone will tell the customer that it's going to help him get rich. Do you now see the power of a good book title? A good title provides instant credibility even before the customer reads the first page!

Even a worthless book with a good title will sell more copies than a book full of useful information with a bad title. And you can quote me on that!

For any non-fiction book, the book title (or subtitle) must immediately tell them what results the book will give them.

Make sure your book title answers the readers question WIIFM if your book is non-fiction. And even for fiction books, it can still be an important piece to choosing a best-selling title.

MYSTERY

Another important feature of a good book title is mystery. Mystery is more important for fiction than non-fiction but it can still be very useful for non-fiction.

For example, Think and Grow Rich has quite a bit of mystery to it. Even though the title makes you believe you will learn how to get rich, you must immediately be wondering questions like,

"Well how is thinking going to help me get rich?"

"Is thinking really what I need to get rich?"

"How rich is the author?"

...and a host of other questions about what the book is going to offer you.

Notice that every question you have about the book based on the title presupposes that the book will help you get rich. You ALREADY assume that the book will help you get rich – now you're just wondering HOW! That's the mystery – and the ONLY WAY to solve that mystery is to buy the book and read it!

This is, I believe, the most powerful combination for a best-selling non-fiction book – a title that tells the reader what's in it for them and then gets the reader to think about the mystery of how it works and buy the book to find out!

FICTION TITLES

Lulu.com has a great tool for analyzing potential book titles and giving you a "percent chance of becoming a best-seller." The tool is based on a study done by Lulu of over 700 best-selling novels and it's incredibly accurate for predicting the success of novel titles.

You can access the tool here lulu.com/titlescorer/index.php

To use it, simply type in the potential title of your book and pick the correct options from the drop-down menus that best describe your book.

Although the tool is meant for novelists, I've found it incredibly useful for nonfiction authors like myself as well. There are universal principles that determine what makes an attractive book title regardless of the genre.

According to Lulu's study of best-selling novels, the title "Sleeping Murder" is the best book title ever written with an 83% probability of becoming a best-seller.

Why is this title so powerful?

Again, I believe, because of the WIIFM/mystery combination. You know the book is about murder so anyone interested in murder mysteries or thrillers will be immediately interested. Second, there's quite a bit of mystery to it (as there is in most good fiction titles).

TITLE LENGTH

The Lulu study found that title length does NOT effect a book's likelihood of becoming a best-seller. This means you can have a short title or a long title or something in between. The key is whether or not the title catches the reader's interest and gives them that inner urge to buy it to satisfy their curiosity.

A great copywriter and marketing expert once told me that any headline you write should be as short as possible while still communicating the whole message. I believe book titles are the same way, with the exception that for Kindle books you want to add some keywords in your title if at all possible to improve search traffic internally from Amazon as well as from Google and other search engines.

THE PROCESS OF CHOOSING A TITLE

Choosing a title for your book should be a process NOT a procedure. A process takes time. It takes iteration after iteration. You'll probably have several working titles before you finally settle on the right one for your book. A procedure is something you do just once and it's over with. That's not how choosing a best-selling book title works most of the time!

Are there instances of an immediate perfect book title coming to an author like Archimedes' Eureka moment in the bathtub? Absolutely! But they are few and far between.

Don't worry about your book title! You WILL find the right title if you put your mind to it and take your time.

Take out a piece of paper or your journal and just write down some possible book titles. Typical of early brainstorming, you should not discard any possible titles at this stage – just let the potential titles flow onto the paper. At this stage, it's good not just to think of titles but also phrases and keywords that could be good. For example, "How to sell more books," "Become a best-seller" and "book business guru" all came to mind when I first started brainstorming the title for this book.

Many best-selling authors now recommend that you think of the title BEFORE you even write the book. I think this is complete bullshit to be quite honest with you.

For self-published writers like you and me, we don't need to worry about finding the perfect title before writing our book. What we need to worry about is writing the book and getting that part done first and foremost!

Why?

Because I've found in my personal experience and in working with hundreds of self-published authors that the biggest obstacle we have to our success is actually writing the book. We procrastinate, delay, put it off and blame "writer's block" for our lack of progress.

Don't let finding the right book title be another stumbling block to your success! Write the book NOW and get it done with. There's always time to figure out the right title. Choosing a book title is a creative process in itself just like writing the book, and it will take time to unfold.

FRICTIONLESS WRITING

I first learned this lesson in the world of blogging. I had been blogging for years and noticed I would have very large "dry spells" – sometimes a month or two would go by without having written a single blog post or article. How could that be? What was stopping me? I was so frustrated! I thought I had to wait for inspiration to hit me.

That's when I listened to an interview with Leo Babauta, founder of the Zen Habits blog (one of the most successful blogs in the world). Leo talked about "frictionless blogging." Frictionless blogging is when you simply write the shell of the blog post and immediately post it live on your site without any pictures, editing, graphics or even formatting. Then, since it's live on your site and people are reading it, it forces you to immediately format it, edit it, add pictures and make it complete. It FORCES you to finish the project – because suddenly your fear of what readers will think of you overcomes your old habits of procrastination and "writer's block."

Since then, I've been using frictionless blogging and it has dramatically improved my results as a blogger. And now I've started what I call frictionless publishing (I believe I'm the first person to apply the concept to this arena but I could be wrong about that). For frictionless publishing, I write the book, finish the chapters and then post it on Kindle with minimal or no editing immediately for 99 cents. At this stage, the book is definitely worth at least 99 cents so I know that anyone who reads it will get a lot of value out of it and will NOT be disappointed in their investment.

But, I don't aim to publish and sell 99 cent books. I believe my books are much more valuable. So as soon as I know the book is live on Kindle, I work my butt off to make sure and edit out all the typos, add in any graphics or pictures I need to, check the formatting, rewrite any sections that are unclear, add in bonus info and content for my readers and voila! What used to take me 2-3 months to edit and complete a book now takes 2-3 days, sometimes less. Once I'm confident that the book is finished and I've uploaded the final copy on Kindle (unless I find more typos or decide to add more later which I can do anytime thanks to the ease of Ebook publishing), I raise the book's price to my ideal selling price.

HOW TO STOP WRITING

Another huge writing tip that has improved my writing output I learned from Tim Ferriss. He recommends that you should ALWAYS stop writing mid-sentence. Why? Because it's much easier to finish a half-written sentence than to start a new one from scratch. And as soon as you finish that first sentence, the second one just flows, and then the third and before you know it you've written a few thousand words and you never wasted a moment wondering what you should write about next.

I highly recommend that whenever you stop writing for the day, stop with a half-written sentence so you can just pick it up where you left off without any hesitation or time wasting.

This new habit will be especially helpful for those of you who, like me, struggle to be consistent with your writing productivity.

CHOOSING A BOOK TITLE SUMMARY

14

Sometimes you will get an instant flash of insight and find the perfect book title in a second. Other times it will take you days, weeks or even months to find the right title for your book. Don't worry – it's all part of the creative process!

I'll tell you what though – you're a lot more likely to come up with a working book title when your book is completed or near completed than when you haven't even written a single word!

ACTION STEPS

Spend 20-30 minutes brainstorming some possible best-selling book titles. After your time is up, keep your notebook or journal near your bed and be open to new book titles and ideas coming to you.

Ask your business or marketing friends for advice on a good book title and other aspects of marketing. If you don't know any good marketers, find one, buy them lunch and take notes.

In the meantime, go back to writing! Writing is the most important creative process and the one you should be spending most of your time on. If your writing is good and you follow the ideas in this book, you'll find your best-selling book title will just come to you when you're ready.

CHAPTER 2. HOW TO MASTER KINDLE CATEGORIES TO SELL MORE BOOKS

Very few authors ever really think about the categories in which they place their Kindle books. Amazon only allows you to choose two categories for your book so you ought to choose wisely. The good thing is that you can change your category choices any time you want (hint: if you want to sell more books, try changing your categories!). Your category choice will have a HUGE impact on your sales!

In fact, choosing the right categories has helped me take books that were only selling 10 or 20 copies a month to over 100-200 copies a month! That's a 10x increase in sales, just by choosing different categories.

Is category selection the magic element to success in Kindle publishing? No – there is no silver bullet or "one magic secret" that will make you successful. It's a combination of several factors – most importantly, the quality of your book and book title! No matter how good your marketing, if your book sucks I doubt you're going to achieve much success with it (although I'm sure we could all find exceptions to this rule).

But, all else being equal, choosing your categories correctly can dramatically increase your sales.

How is it possible that such a small thing like changing a category can have such a huge impact on your book sales?

First of all, you have to realize how most Kindle readers find books in the first place. They generally browse and skim – and categories are the most common way readers browse for new books, after using Amazon search. The problem, though, for new authors and new books especially is that readers generally only browse the top 10 or 20 books in a category. This means that if you're #87 in your category, you're very unlikely to get any sales because of your category listing. On the other hand, if you choose a category that you don't even rank in, you won't get any sales from your category!

Okay so think of it this way. Let's say your book now sells 30 copies a month. Your book is about investing in stocks and it's listed in the Business & Investing category. The problem is that book #100 in that category is ranked #5,027 in the paid Kindle store books, meaning it sells about 30 copies a day! Therefore, your listing in that category is completely worthless because Amazon will not show your book in that category listing, meaning you won't get any sales from it (If you're not in the top #100 in your category, Amazon won't even list you in that category).

Therefore, for a book selling less than 30 copies a day, choosing the Business & Investing for one of your two categories will add a grand total of 0 sales a month. This means one of your most effective marketing strategies (your book's category) isn't doing ANY marketing for you at all! That's when you know it's time to do a category change (assuming you already sell at least 1 or 2 books a month).

You won't be selling any additional books in a category if you're not in the top 100. So what can you do instead of leaving it in a category where you can't yet rank in the top 100?

The answer is simple: Choose a category in which you CAN rank in the top 100 (or preferably top 10!) so that you can attract more browsers and buyers for your book in that category.

AN EXAMPLE

As an example, my book The Blog Business Book wasn't selling nearly enough copies to reach the top 100 in either of my preferred categories: Web Marketing and Blogging. So what to do?

I chose a related category instead which was much easier to rank for:

Kindle Store > Kindle books > Nonfiction > Business & Investing > Marketing & Sales > Marketing > **Direct**

Like I said earlier, I'd rather be #60 in Direct than not have any ranking at all in Blogging. When sales increase and the book joins the top 10 in the Direct Category, I'll switch it over to Blogging where it will then rank well in that category. This is how you can "jump" from a smaller category to a larger category to sell more books – but don't even try it until you get into the top 20 in the smaller category!

THE AMAZON CATEGORY NIGHTMARE!

For any of you who've already gone through the process of picking categories for your book, you know how incredibly confusing it can be. First of all, Amazon organizes their categories with little if any logic. To make matters even more complicated, the categories you choose when you're uploading your book to Amazon don't even match the categories Amazon shows on your book page!

Furthermore, Amazon changes their categories and listings very often. Because of this, I'm not able to tell you the best category for your specific book even though I would love to be that helpful. Unfortunately, if I compiled such a list, it would be out of date by the time it was uploaded to Kindle! Categories change frequently over time and you need to be able to figure it out on your own. Just use the guidelines in this chapter and you'll do fine.

To make things even more complicated, Amazon will change your book category in an instant if it thinks it has a better match for you. Like it did with this book! For some reason, Amazon thought my book on Kindle marketing should be placed in the Accounting category:

Product Details
File Size: 490 KB
Sold by: Amazon Digital Services, Inc.
Language: English
ASIN: B00A86QV9A
Text-to-Speech: Enabled
X-Ray: Not Enabled
Lending: Enabled
Amazon Best Sellers Rank: #4,700 Paid in Kindle Store (See Top 100 Paid in Kindle Store)
    #3 in Kindle Store > Kindle eBooks > Nonfiction > Business & Investing > Marketing & Sales > Advertising
    #4 in Books > Business & Investing > Marketing & Sales > Advertising
    #4 in Books > Business & Investing > Accounting

Did we miss any relevant features for this product? Tell us what we missed.
Would you like to give feedback on images or tell us about a lower price?

Also notice how my book is now in two different "Advertising" categories. How does that even work? One section is for "books" which includes physical as well as ebooks. The other is just for the Kindle store which only includes ebooks.

Amazon can and will change your categories at any given time. I had originally chosen different categories for my book, but, Amazon in its infinite wisdom has changed them. So what can you do about it?

Just login to Amazon KDP at kdp.amazon.com, scroll down to the very bottom of the page and hit the Contact Us link at the bottom right of the page next to Conditions & Use. Then, click "Product Page" and type your email in the box. They'll get back to you within 24 hours and are always very helpful in my experience.

Here's a sample email to write asking Amazon to change a category to a more appropriate one:

"Hello,

My book [insert name of your book] is now listed in [insert category name you'd like to change] and I feel it would more appropriately fit in [pick your ideal category] – can you please tell me why this change was made and help me fix it?

Thanks!

[Your Name]"

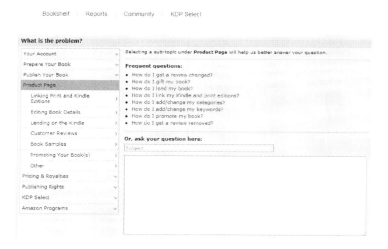

The KDP Help box on the other page is how you will contact Amazon support for any technical issues with your Kindle books.

Also notice that my book appears in three categories even though Amazon only allows you to choose two categories when you upload it. Well, Amazon has larger, more competitive general categories and it will lump your book into those if it is selling well. It auto-assigns them based on unknown factors. So, if your book is selling well, you might get three category rankings instead of two.

This is actually the reason I contacted Amazon, because if I go back and manually change my categories again, Amazon will remove the third listing sometimes and I want my book to stay in three categories to improve sales.

FREE PROMO CATEGORIES

During a KDP free promo, it's best to choose your IDEAL category first and foremost, regardless of the competition. There are separate category rankings for paid and free Kindle books and even the most competitive paid Kindle book category has a corresponding free Kindle book category that is much, much easier to rank for.

So when you're doing your KDP free promotion, choose your ideal categories and see how your free downloads do. If you're not getting enough downloads to rank in the top 10 in any category, change your categories so that you can rank in the top 10 during your free promotion.

If you go through your entire free promotion without making a top 10 in any category, you've missed out on a HUGE opportunity to get thousands of downloads very quickly.

You'll learn a lot more about how to launch a successful KDP free promotion in Chapter 10.

HOT NEW RELEASES AND TOP RATED BOOKS

There are two special category sections on the top right side of each category page that will get your book an extra listing on your category page. They're called the Hot New Releases and Top Rated section of each category and three books will be featured in each.

I was pleasantly surprised to see this very book reach the Hot New Releases section in the Advertising category.

Notice that this book appears in two spots above the fold in the advertising category – it's #3 in the paid category overall and it's in the Hot New Releases section. You want to aim for a category that you can get in the top 10 like this and do it as fast as possible so that your book also reaches the Hot New Releases section. This will help you get more sales early on.

This particular book started selling about 10 copies a day on average for a week before it made the Hot New Releases section. That's only 70 books in the first week! Although it may sound like a lot for new self-published authors, when you follow the systems and strategies in this book, I think you'll find it much more doable. If you're struggling to sell copies in the first week of your release, try lowering the price to 99 cents to make it more appealing to readers and aim for that Hot New Releases category – you can then raise your price and often maintain the sales ranking.

As for the Top Rated section, you pretty much have to have a perfect 5-star rating to make it there. Most books in this section in major categories have 30-100 ratings with 90% or more of them being 5-stars. So it's not easy to do! You have to have an incredibly well-written book and solicit honest reviews from customers and/or professional reviewers. We'll talk more about how to do that ethically in Chapter 6.

ACTION STEPS

Remember, you can change your category anytime you want. If you're not in the top 100 in a category, change your category to a less competitive one.

Go check your books right now on Amazon Kindle and see where they rank. If they're not in the top 100 in both of your chosen categories, research a less competitive category and change it!

CHAPTER 3. HOW TO SELL MORE BOOKS USING THE RIGHT KEYWORDS AND TAGS

Categories are the second most important way new browsers on Amazon will find your book (unless you reach Amazon's Top 100 overall list). But the largest source of traffic to your book page and sales from Amazon itself will be due to Amazon search.

Luckily, Amazon allows you to have some control over how your book appears in the Amazon Kindle Store search results. You can influence the search results by first of all doing your keyword research and putting your desired search keywords in your book's tags, title and description.

In this chapter we'll cover the exact process you can use for keyword research to choose the keywords that will lead to the most sales and then we'll discuss how to add these keywords to your book's tags.

AMAZON KEYWORD RESEARCH

If you've ever done keyword research before for SEO purposes, this is a very similar process. For those of you who are totally new to SEO (Search Engine Optimization), it's a very simple process and I'm going to walk you through it step-by-step so that you can apply it to your book page to sell more books.

The first thing you must do is keyword research.

STEP 1. GOOGLE KEYWORD RESEARCH

Go to adwords.google.com/o/KeywordTool and search for a general keyword related to your topic. First of all, you will have to login to your Google account if you haven't already.

I'll use this book as an example. One of my keywords, I know, will be "how to sell more kindle books" so I'm going to type that keyword phrase into the Google Keyword Tool:

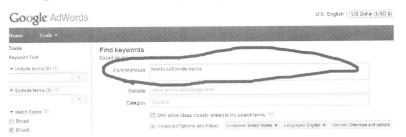

The next thing you must do is click the [Exact] button on the left side of the screen under the "Match Types" category:

It's very important that you use Exact Match when searching for keywords. This tells Google that you want data for EXACT search terms – meaning Google will count the number of times someone typed in the exact words "how to sell more kindle books" – otherwise the data will be skewed with searches related to your search which doesn't help you choose the right keyword.

26

Next, click the "Global Monthly Searches" bar to sort the keyword by the most searched.

With this search, Google gave me the following keywords which I think MIGHT help me sell more books (each of these keywords gets over 1,000 global monthly Exact searches on Google):

how to write a book

how to publish a book

self publishing

sell books online

writing a book

how to get published

kindle self publishing

write a book

selling books online

publish your own book

how to publish an ebook

how to write an ebook

book marketing

how to self publish a book

how to self publish

getting a book published

Now that I've gathered some potential keywords from Google, the next step is to use Amazon search to see which searches Amazon recommends.

Step 2. Amazon Keyword Research

Now that we have our preliminary list of keywords from Google, let's head on over to Amazon.com's Kindle Store search to see what Amazon recommends to searchers.

Make sure you search ONLY in the Amazon Kindle store when doing Amazon keyword research because otherwise your results will be skewed. You can access the Kindle Store only search function here: http://amzn.to/RLGyUr

Once I'm on Amazon's Kindle Store, I'm going to type in my keywords into the search box. Notice how Amazon almost immediately starts recommending keywords and searches to me:

I simply wrote "how to write" and Amazon returned 10 other keywords and search terms including "how to write a book" and "how to write a novel," among others.

This means my keyword "how to write a book" is not only recommended by Google search, it's also recommended by Amazon search! Meaning this is a GREAT keyword and I should definitely consider using this keyword in my book's title, description and tags. Why? Because Amazon browsers AND

29

Google searchers are both using this keyword to search for something – like my book!

STEP 3. KEYWORD RELEVANCE CHECK

The final step for keyword research is very subjective – this is the "art" of keyword research so to speak. My book isn't technically about how to write a book – it's really about how to sell more books on Amazon's Kindle platform.

So if someone types into Amazon's search box "how to write a book" and my book appeared, would they really want to click on it and buy it?

Now, you could argue either way. You could theorize that if someone is trying to figure out how to write a book then they will also want to know how to sell more books on Amazon Kindle and will therefore be very interested in my book. So this is a great keyword!

You could also argue that someone who's searching for "how to write a book" isn't yet ready to learn how to publish on Kindle because they first need to learn how to write their book before they can publish and sell it!

Which argument do you think is better? Should I use that keyword or not to try to attract more book sales?

Want to know my opinion? Check out my book page on Amazon and see if I used the keyword or not in my tags, title and/or book description!

What You Need To Know About Choosing Keywords

You might feel like I'm "leaving something out" here about choosing keywords but I'm not. That's really all you need to know to use them to sell more books. The problem is that there's a huge grey area – the area where your subjective opinion about what Amazon users are searching for meet the objective numbers from the Google Adwords Keyword Tool.

Here's my opinion: If you get stuck trying to choose one keyword over another that you found through either the Google Keyword Tool or Amazon Search suggestions, just choose one. It doesn't matter. Don't get stuck in the nitty gritty. Don't get "paralysis by analysis" as so many of us perfectionists tend to do. At the end of the day, one good keyword is better than not having any keywords at all.

"An imperfect plan today is better than a perfect plan tomorrow." – General George Patton

And the good news is you can always change your keywords later if you change your mind or if the search results change.

Again, I want to caution you about spending too much time on keyword selection. Find your keywords on Google and Amazon, choose 7 or so you think are the best, upload them and be done with it, knowing confidently in your heart that it's better to have mediocre keywords than no keywords. You can always change it later.

How To Add Your Keywords To Your Book

In the past, you used to be able to add keyword tags to your book to help attract more search traffic from within Amazon and Google. Amazon just recently removed tags from all books On January 16, 2013. A friend emailed KDP Select and KDP support said,

"The original idea of Tags was to allow customers to tag items they were considering buying (for example, tagging items for a specific person as a gift), tagging products that they have purchased for later recommendations and tagging products to suggest better organization of them for Amazon.

Over time Amazon has introduced new features that have replaced the Tags functionality, including Wish Lists, Customer Reviews and Recommendations.

Since the introduction of those features the usage of Tags, and therefore their value to our customers, has declined. We have removed Tags in favor of the replacement features. Tags that you created are still available under Your Profile page."

Because tags are no longer functional and they've been replaced with Wish Lists, Reviews and Recommendations, I recommend you focus on getting your customers to recommend your book, review it and add it to their wish list instead.

Once you've completed the above 3-step process and created a list of high quality, relevant keywords for your book, it's time to add your top 7 keywords to your book through your KDP book upload page.

33

How To Add Keywords to Your Book

Step 1. Login to KDP.AMAZON.COM

Step 2. Edit Your Book In Your Bookshelf

Step 3. Add Your 7 Best Keywords

Under "3. Target Your Customers," you'll find your keyword box where you can type in your top 7 keywords.

Make sure you type in the keywords exactly without any spelling errors. Also make sure to separate your keywords with commas. If you misspell your keywords or miss a comma, your keywords won't help you at all!

So your keywords should look like this: how to sell more kindle ebooks, how to sell more books, kindle publishing, etc.

Your 7 Search Keywords

Always remember that if you want to change these 7 search keywords at any time, just edit your book and you can change them. I recommend testing out your keywords for at least two weeks and then checking your search rankings in Amazon. Just search for each keyword separately in Amazon search and see where you rank! If you're ranking in the top 3, that's awesome! It means you will definitely get sales from that keyword.

If you're ranked in the top 10, that's good. Try adding that keyword to your book description as well to raise your ranking.

If you're not ranking in the top 10 after two weeks for one of your tags, I would recommend changing your tag to something else so that you can rank in the top 10, or preferably, top 3. This way, your tags will help you get more sales rather than just taking up space.

SEARCH EXAMPLE

I want to give you an example of keyword searches in Amazon's Kindle store so you can get a feel for how it works. I searched for "love" and received 77,727 results! That's a LOT of competition for that keyword – which should be expected because it's such a common word and it's a one-word keyword. Keyword phrases with multiple words will be naturally less competitive – and more conducive to increasing your sales.

Next, I searched for "How To Love A Pet" and Amazon only gave me 14 results for this search, meaning it's MUCH less competitive and easier to rank highly for.

Notice that the keyword phrase "How to love a pet" is so much more targeted and narrowed down than the general keyword "love." It's a lot more specific. Remember that someone who types "love" into a search box might just be browsing or researching – but someone who types in a specific phrase like "how to write an ebook" is much more likely to be a buyer because they're looking for something very specific.

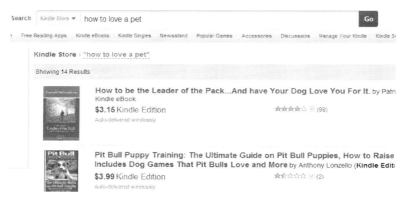

Ideally, you want high quality, relevant keywords for your tags that are also not highly competitive. How do you know if it's highly competitive? Well, the easiest way is to just check your own search results for your keywords after 2-3 weeks on Amazon. Does your book come up in the top 10 or farther down the list? If your book is in the top 10, congratulations! You're likely to get sales from that keyword if it's well-chosen. If you're much farther down then you may need to wait longer for your book to rise up in the search results because of stronger competition.

36

Note: This is just my opinion from my own experience and countless hours spent analyzing Amazon search results, but I believe that Amazon, unlike other search engines, ranks search results not just by "keyword relevance" but also by sales rankings. What does that mean? Well, Amazon wants to sell more books so they have a part of their search results algorithm that calculates how many copies your book has sold and compares it to others in the search results. The bottom line is that if you sell more books, your search results in Amazon will improve over time. This benefits Amazon because they sell more books and it benefits you because you sell more books when you follow the strategies in this book!

DIFFERENT KEYWORDS FOR DIFFERENT VERSIONS

By the way, different versions of a book will have different keywords when you upload them. For example, a book published in paperback via CreateSpace as well as Kindle will have different and separate keywords for the paperback sales page and the Kindle sales page. So make sure you utilize good relevant and DIFFERENT keywords for each version of your book!

ACTION STEPS

Do your keyword research for Google and Amazon and add your researched, targeted keywords to your book.

CHAPTER 4. DESIGNING A BEST-SELLING BOOK COVER

Your book cover is one of the most important pieces to your marketing strategy. You can appear in all the search results you want but people won't click on your book if the cover looks awful or confusing or communicates something other than what you want.

For example, look at the following two cover designs I found for two books about puppy training. Which do you prefer? Which do you think sells more copies?

The first book sells over 30 copies a day. The second book sells less than 10 a month. Pretty big difference, huh?

Of course, you couldn't say that the only difference is the cover. It's not. But I'm sure you felt an immediate difference looking at one cover from the other. Why?

The first cover looks incredibly professional. The picture of the dog is adorable and immediately lets you know it's about puppies. The star design makes it look unconsciously like the book received an award of some kind. It just looks and feels like a book cover you would see on the NY Times best-sellers list or at your local bookstore, doesn't it?

But the second cover looks like some 12 year old made it with Photoshop or Paint (not that I have anything against ambitious 12 year olds).

You see, book readers make emotional decisions (as all buyers do) about whether or not to buy your book. If your cover looks unprofessional, you're out! When a customer sees a poorly designed cover, they think, "Why waste money and time on a book when the author can't even get a good looking cover?"

Out of every area where you could spend money on your book, I believe the cover is the most important by far. It will have the single biggest impact on your sales. The good news is you can get an excellent, professional cover designed for less than $250. And for those of you on a budget, you can get it done for just $5!

GETTING A PROFESSIONAL COVER DESIGNER

You can hire a professional cover designer to do a custom ebook cover for anywhere from $200 to $1,000 or more.

Here are some sites that provide high quality ebook cover designs in this price range:

www.authorsupport.com

www.booktango.com (Provides a lot more marketing and editing support in addition to custom cover design)

www.bookcoverdesignbyindigo.com

www.ebookcoverdesignsbycarey.com

www.damonza.com

www.gobookcoverdesign.com (Robin is my favorite designer for paperback books and does incredible work for $80 to $240 for paperback covers. She also designs ebook covers, of course).

Design Contests

If you don't just want one designer but instead would like to see hundreds of potential designs and choose the best, I recommend going with 99designs.com

99designs allows you to create a contest where hundreds of graphic designers compete to design the best book cover (or t-shirt or whatever you want designed) just for you according to your criteria! Then you choose the best design and use that.

Prices range from $149 to $279.

The Economical Route

For those on a tight budget, you can use Fiverr.com to find some good cover designers who will do the job for just $5. But rather than make you waste your time looking around for the right Fiverr cover designer, I'm just going to share with you the one I use: http://bit.ly/UkbZ5e

He designs 3d ebook covers as well for websites so just make sure you tell him you want a flat cover for your Amazon Kindle ebook.

Here's an example of one of the covers he designed for me:

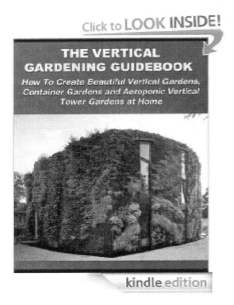

Not only that, but he also designed the book cover for this book! It looks like this:

Not bad for $5, huh?

So how do you get someone to design a great cover for you for just $5? Well, first of all, they have to be a skilled designer. But secondly, you have to give them very clear instructions.

What color do you want it to be?

What words do you want to appear on the cover? (Generally, the Title, subtitle and Author's name)

What kind of picture(s) do you want? Is the designer responsible for coming up with the pictures or do you have some already in mind?

What I Recommend

For brand new authors on a tight budget, I recommend getting a well-designed $5 cover and seeing how it goes, especially if you have several books. You can always upgrade to a $250 cover anytime you want.

Let's say you have 5 books and one of them is outselling the others hands-down – then you should first design a $250 cover for that book that's selling more. Once your profits from your royalties are enough, you can pay for newer, better covers for all your books.

Testing Ebook Covers

I highly recommend testing all of your ebook covers! You never know which is the best cover until you test it. The good news is it's now easier than ever to test.

There's a very simple way you can test which book covers convert better with a few dollars and a Facebook Ads account.

STEP 1. CREATE FACEBOOK ADS ACCOUNT

Go to Facebook.com/ads and create a Facebook ads account. You will need a credit card and a personal Facebook account to do so.

STEP 2. CREATE ADS

Next, create a Facebook ad for each of your potential covers. Leave the text in the ad and the headline exactly the same. The ONLY difference in the ads should be the covers. Make sure the targeting and demographics and ad bid is exactly the same, otherwise the results will be skewed.

STEP 3. CHECK RESULTS

Check the results of your ads after anywhere from 2-7 days depending on your budget and targeting options you selected. Whichever ad had the highest CTR (Click-Through Rate) is the best ad – it means that book cover image pulled more clicks than the others per every impression on Facebook.

ACTION STEPS

Decide what your budget is for your book cover. Got extra cash? Go for a professional designer.

Budget tight? Then just go the Fiverr route for now.

44

Make sure to **test your book covers** using Facebook ads before finalizing payment to your designer! Let your designer know ahead of time you will be testing the cover and will not provide final payment until you're sure it's the best one.

CHAPTER 5. WRITING YOUR BOOK DESCRIPTION

Writing a good book description is one of the most important things you can do to increase your book sales.

For those of you who are familiar with SEO, writing an Amazon Kindle book description is like crafting the content for the "on-page SEO" of any web page. Basically, Amazon (and Google) indexes your book's page and takes special note of the words in your book description and title.

Any keywords you include inside your book description, therefore, will make your book much more likely to appear in Amazon (and Google) search results when someone types in that keyword. So if you want more sales from Amazon search results, it just makes sense to use as many of your targeted keywords as possible in the description without "keyword stuffing." Keyword stuffing is a term used in SEO for just writing keywords over and over instead of readable text.

I highly recommend NOT keyword stuffing! Google already penalizes this tactic and I'm sure Amazon is not far behind. Plus, any reader with common sense will probably avoid a book when the description ends with the oh-so-moving and memorable line, "how to write a book, how to publish a book self-publishing sell books online writing a book how to get published kindle self-publishing write a book selling books online publish your own book how to publish an ebook how to write an ebook book marketing how to self-publish a book how to self-publish getting a book published."

How To Use Keywords In Your Book Description

Amazon gives you 4,000 characters you can use to write your book description which equates to about 600-700 words. You ought to be able to include 6-7 primary keyword phrases in your description with no problem from Google or other search engines – and still have the description sound engaging and meaningful for the reader to devour.

When you start writing your book description, I recommend ignoring keywords to start. Just let your thoughts flow and write good, engaging sales copy using as many of the 4,000 characters as you can. The keyword here is SALES COPY – you must be able to write copy that SELLS your book. Using the techniques in this book, you will learn how to get thousands of new Amazon browsers who will see your book page and book Title. If the title is engaging they will likely read your description. But if your book description does not make them want to buy your book (selling), few of those extra eyeballs will turn into sales for you.

If you have never written sales copy before or are unsure how to, I highly recommend reading *The Adweek Copywriting Handbook* by Joseph Sugarman. In the book, he shares everything he learned in over 40 years of writing copy for national advertisements and his own large marketing company.

Why You Must Sell Your Book

Many authors, I know, are disgusted by selling. They don't want anything to do with sales or manipulation tactics. But that's not what selling is about!

47

Sales is about helping the potential customer understand that you have the solution to their problem. When it comes to nonfiction books, it is extremely important that you not only identify but communicate to the customer what problem your book will help them solve.

Often, it's quite simple really. For example, this book helps authors like you solve the problem of selling more books on Amazon Kindle. See how specific it is? It's not about selling physical books (although almost the every piece of advice in here is applicable to that arena) and it's not even about just selling ebooks in general. It's a very specific problem being solved by this book for a very specific group of people just like you!

Therefore, my book description must CLEARLY let potential buyers know that my book will help you dramatically increase your sales of Amazon Kindle books. It must also help overcome objections that the customer might have. For example, a potential buyer of this book might think, "I've tried using social media to promote my books and it didn't work!" so I've got to let these potential customers know that they DON'T need to do anything with social media to be successful in selling A LOT more Kindle books.

There are many other potential objections as well that I cover in the book description. Write down what you think could be potential objections from your book customers. What problems might you be able to anticipate that you can solve even before they buy the book?

FICTION BOOK DESCRIPTIONS

When it comes to fiction, this whole problem-solution is not as clear. Most often, people read fiction for entertainment. Therefore, your book description must provide them with entertainment! The description ITSELF must be entertaining or else why bother buying a novel from an unknown author with no publisher?

You see, a fiction book description should immediately involve the reader in the plot. And, like a good book title, the description should leave a bit of mystery lurking in the reader's mind and the only way to solve that mystery is... you guessed it! Buy your book!

BEST SELLING AUTHOR VS. BEST WRITING AUTHOR

When I was 19 years old, I read Robert Kiyosaki's book *Rich Dad Poor Dad* and in the book he talks about a conversation he had with a journalist and wannabe author where he had to explain to her the difference between being a best-selling author and a best-writing author. You see, a best-writing author can easily go broke and suffer from no-readers-itis. But a best-selling author is not necessarily a best-writing author. On the contrary, a best-selling author is someone who understands what readers want and need (the problem) and helps them solve that problem – before they even read the book!

You see, your book title, description and cover must be so informative, educational and moving that it inspires people to buy it – or else you will never become a best-selling author.

Special HTML Formatting For Your Book Description

Amazon allows you to insert basic HTML in your book descriptions. The problem? Most authors don't know HTML first of all.

But there's another problem that makes it even more complex – Amazon uses a weird HTML system where instead of using < and > they use < and > (lt standing for less than and gt standing for greater than).

Because you're reading this on a Kindle device which makes it difficult if not impossible to copy and paste text, I've written a blog post that explains exactly how you can use custom Amazon HTML tags in your book descriptions to make them stand out.

Using these HTML codes you can create headlines, insert images, use bold, italics and underlined text, center and justify your text and even use the Amazon Orange headlines in your book descriptions.

Even if you have NO IDEA what HTML is or how to use it, all you have to do is read the short blog post and copy and paste the HTML codes into your book description to make it stand out and look way better than your competitors' book descriptions.

You can read the entire article on my blog with step-by-step instructions here: http://bit.ly/UMmJK2

Chapter 6. How To Get More Reviews (The Ethical Way) And How To Handle Bad Reviews

The only thing worse for your book sales than having no reviews is having a 1-star or 2-star rating.

The problem is that only 1 in 1,000 book readers will actually leave a review on Amazon – meaning you would have to sell 1,000 books before you would get even a single review! The problem with this for new self-published authors is that you will NEVER get 1,000 book sales unless you have good reviews for your book. So it's the whole chicken before the egg dilemma.

Should you focus on selling a thousand books so you can get your first reviews or should you focus on getting reviews so you can sell a few thousand books?

Personally, I recommend going after reviews as soon as your book is published to help you sell more books. Here's how to do it ethically!

How To Get More Reviews

Some authors will tell you it's unethical to ask your friends, family and colleagues to review your books. That's bogus! It's only unethical when positive reviews are paid for or given in return for something else, or when reviews are made without disclosing the relationship between the author and the reviewer.

For example, if your mom writes you a 5-star review for your book, she should say that she is your mom in the review. For example, she could leave you a 5-star review and write something like this:

"This is the best book on how to sell more Kindle books I've ever read! Well, the truth is it's the only book I've ever read on the subject because my son wrote it. But I really think new and existing authors alike would enjoy this book and find it very useful. I know that my son has been able to earn a full-time income using these techniques and strategies and I'm very proud of him."

Is it cheesy? Yes. But it's also honest, sincere and ethical. And it will help you get more sales because books with no reviews or negative reviews are very hard to sell. But a book with just one 5-star review will sell 3 to 4 times as many copies as a book with no reviews in my experience.

By the way, this is the way book reviews have always been solicited from the author's friends - or, more specifically, from the colleagues and friends of the publisher. Sometimes they call themselves "professional book reviewers." But in the publishing industry, they're really just paid to review books so that the publishers can sell more of them.

This is why every hot new best-selling book ALWAYS has plenty of reviews inside the book itself and on the back cover before it's even "sold" a single copy. How else would that be possible without the help of others who have a biased relationship with the author and/or publisher?

The simple truth of the matter is that you need good reviews to sell more books. And the only way to get good reviews in the beginning is to ask other people to review your book. Whether they are friends, family, business partners or random people you find in online chat rooms doesn't really matter. What matters is that you get the reviews in an ethical manner and that they add meaningful information to prospective buyers.

A SHORTCUT FOR GETTING REVIEWS

Amazon has a list of the top 500 and top 1000 reviewers. I highly recommend contacting these top reviewers and asking them to review your book!

However, just trying to find each top reviewer on the Amazon site and find out if they're even interested in reading books in your niche or genre can be, quite honestly, a frustrating waste of time. I know because I tried it!

But then I learned a brilliant shortcut that I'm going to share with you that I learned from the book *Secret Amazon Hacks and Other Cool Tricks For Kindle Authors.*

All you have to do is go to Google.com and type the following into the search box:

"top 1000 reviewer" "your niche or genre" "e-mail:" site:http://www.amazon.com/gp/pdp/profile

(Want to copy and paste this code? You can copy it from my blog here: http://bit.ly/TkyuYJ)

When you type in the code and search for it, you'll get results like this:

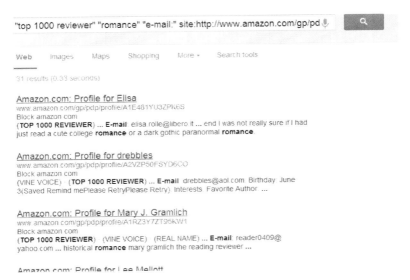

Notice that Google has returned 31 Top 1000 Amazon reviewers with the word "Romance" in their profile who also have their email listed in their profile. If I had written a romance novel, I know I'd be emailing these folks and asking for a review!

Most top ranked reviewers welcome review requests and thoroughly love being a professional reviewer. Treat them like a professional and they will provide you with an invaluable service.

Just remember to follow Amazon's Guidelines for reviews and ethics.

How To Handle Bad Reviews

Positive reviews help you sell more books. But negative reviews are dramatically more powerful in that a single 1-star review can tank your sales instantly!

So what should you do if you suddenly get a 1-star review for your brand new book and your sales plummet?

54

Well, it all depends on the review!

But I believe the best defense is a good offense. And when it comes to Kindle publishing, that means you need to get good reviews first and foremost so that you'll be protected against any one negative review from a customer who's got a chip on their shoulder or an unethical, slimy competitor who's just trying to tear you down.

I really can't reiterate this point enough – you NEED good reviews in order to sell a lot of books. Period.

This is the step-by-step process I take when it comes to handling negative reviews.

How To Handle Negative Reviews

It's always fun to see when readers review your books and get some great feedback and acknowledgment for all your hard work.

After you do a free KDP promotion for your book, you will likely get several reviews naturally. But what do you do if someone leaves you a nasty, negative 1-star or 2-star review?

Well, there are a few options. First you have to understand where the review is coming from.

Is it an honest review from an irate customer or does it appear to be a shill review from a nasty competitor who's trying to kill your book sales?

Many times when your book receives a negative review the reviewer will leave some very helpful information that can help you improve the book, especially for new authors.

Maybe your formatting is off or there are lots of typos or there's missing information or some information is unclear. Whatever the problem, the negative review will help you notice the problem so that you can fix it and make your book even better. I really can't overstate the importance of this – you MUST learn from your customer reviews so that you can IMPROVE your work as an author. This is how good authors become GREAT authors – by learning from their mistakes and from readers.

So it's actually a good thing to get an honest negative review if it helps you improve the book! Of course, if it's the ONLY review you get, it can dramatically hurt your sales which is why getting reviews ahead of time is so important to prevent any chance of your sales tanking from just one bad review.

If you do get a negative, honest review from an upset customer, just brush it off. Learn what you can from the review, improve your book, and move on. It's okay to down vote the negative review. Just click the "No" button next to "Was this review helpful to you?" – that way the review will hopefully be pushed down below the other, more positive reviews.

But what do you do if you get a shill negative review from someone who obviously never read your book and is probably an author of a competitive book who's just posting garbage so they can kill your book sales in order to sell more books of their own?

Well, first of all, these kinds of reviews do happen more often than they should due to unscrupulous authors who have a very poor ethical code. So if you find you've received a shill negative review, here's what to do:

REPORT THE REVIEW

You can report the review (Just click "Report Abuse" under the review) and it will notify Amazon of a review that breaks the Amazon Terms of Service (TOS). Generally, if you suspect another author has left a negative review disguised on a fake account you should report it.

You can also...

THUMBS DOWN THE REVIEW

You can hit the "No" button under the question "Was this review helpful?" to let Amazon know it wasn't helpful. This will help push the review down below the top 3 most helpful reviews so that less people see it.

You can also ask your customers, friends, fellow authors and family to report reviews that break Amazon's TOS. If Amazon receives enough reports, they will likely remove the shill review (as they should!). Amazon is a company based on trust and they are usually very proactive about fake reviews (as proactive as a multi-billion dollar company can be).

Next, you can...

Respond To The Review

Lastly, you can respond to the review. This is the path I took when a fake Amazon profile reviewed my book. I noticed that the link in the profile was to a website that was owned by a company that owns several pornographic websites – red flag right there. (I found this information by checking the WhoIs database and by running a basic Google search for the company that owned the website linked in the Amazon profile).

I then simply responded to the review stating that I had found that information and that my book was for bloggers not for people who run pornographic sites. This way at least readers will understand where that review came from (the reviewer seemed to be angry that my book on blogging strongly urged readers to avoid linking to pornographic sites). Go figure!

Once you've taken these basic steps, it's time to…

Let It Go

At the end of the day you've just got to let it go. Don't get upset over negative reviews – they happen. Even the most popular books in the world receive HUNDREDS of 1-star and 2-star reviews. You can't please everyone all the time. So don't worry about it!

If you're not receiving harsh criticism about your books then I can guarantee you aren't selling very many! There's always going to be someone who doesn't like your writing style, personality, advice, ideas or stories – that's okay. Not everyone is just like you. The key is to understand that as more and more readers enjoy your work and come to love you, there will be others who read your work and come to not like you. That's just how it is.

Look at our current President of the United States, Barack Obama. Some people love him and some people hate him. Yet he's one of the most powerful men in the world. The same goes for George Bush, Bill Clinton and every other president in the history of the United States. Some love 'em, some hate 'em. So what? That's the life of a president – and a successful author.

My advice to you is this: just keep writing and go about your business. That's how you create lasting success as an author. Why write a detailed response to a negative review when you put all that creative energy and time into writing your next bestseller?

Don't focus on the detractors, haters and unethical authors. They can only stop you from the success you dream of if you let them!

CHAPTER 7. CALCULATING KINDLE SALES ESTIMATES

It can be very useful when doing market research or dreaming and planning about your future royalties to understand the Kindle sales ranking system and how that translates into sales.

Here's a great site that will tell you how many copies are sold each day for a given sales rank: kdpcalculator.com

Another good site is novelrank.com

Neither of these sites are 100% accurate, but they will give you a good idea of how many books are being sold (your own books and competitors' books for market research).

HOW TO USE SALES RANK DATA

Most often, I use sales rank data for category selection. For example, if I see my book's sales rank is #50,000 and I want to be in the top 10 of the Blogging & Blogs category on Amazon, then I go and see what the sales ranks are for the top 10 books in the Blogging & Blogs category.

Right now as I'm writing at my desk, the #1 book in this category is Planet Tad at #3,287 in the Kindle store. The #10 book in the category is ProBlogger at #10,716 in the Kindle store. So I know my book won't be in the top 10 if I switch categories... but what rank would it be at in that category?

Well I check more books in the Blogging & Blogs category and notice that Blogging Tips is #58 in the category with a

Kindle sales rank of #50,293 – very close to my book's sales rank. So I know my book will rank around #57 or so in that category.

Cool, huh?

Using this strategy and data, you can research what categories your book will be able to rank in and how well it will rank before choosing the category.

CHAPTER 8. WHAT YOU NEED TO KNOW ABOUT INTERNATIONAL KINDLE SALES

One of the things I noticed very quickly in The Society is that some of our authors came from the US and some from the UK – and that Amazon has a completely separate website for both countries! This means totally separate reviews, categories, tag, keywords, likes and sales prices!

When I first started publishing Kindle books, I noticed that my UK sales were about 10% of my US sales – representing a good amount of income and a nice diversity of currency I was getting paid in. But, at the end of the day, UK sales were not significant enough to warrant investing time and energy into focusing on increasing my UK marketing. Or was it?

I decided to test it.

I noticed that my US Kindle book might have 40 likes, 13 reviews and 20 tags while that same book listing in the UK had zero reviews, zero tags and only 2 or 3 likes. I wondered if the reason my UK sales were so low was simply because of these factors and not the size or willingness of the market to buy my books?

So I started using the same strategies mentioned earlier in this book about adding tags, likes and ethical reviews and I noticed a funny thing happened – my UK sales went from 10% of my US sales to 17% in one month!

Now that's not life-changing money right there for most authors but it is a significant increase in sales and royalties for just 1-2 hours of work at most.

The only problem with this strategy is finding UK based reviewers if you don't live in the UK! Luckily for me, The Society had several UK members. So I told them I was conducting a study on the effects of reviews, tags, likes and categories on UK sales vs. US sales and asked them to leave an honest review of the book for me in order to help with the test.

Here are some very important findings I noticed:

REVIEWS

First of all, you don't need nearly as many reviews in the UK as you do in the US. In the US, I noticed that at least 6 reviews were the optimal number to increase sales. After that, the usefulness of each additional review tapered off. Each additional review after the 6th helped increase sales but only a very small amount, whereas the first 6 reviews had a dramatic impact on sales.

In the UK, however, just two positive reviews was all I needed to dramatically increase sales. After that, each additional review tapered off. Bottom line: one or two good UK reviews will do wonders for your UK sales.

CATEGORIES

Categories are less competitive in the UK than in the US – MUCH less competitive. Just by following the advice in this book on choosing the right keywords, you should be able to get into the top 10 or 20 of just about any category except the most competitive.

63

This means you'll have to do your own category research and testing in the UK separate from the US in order to maximize UK sales.

KEYWORDS

Books on the Amazon.co.uk store have different search rankings and results. I recommend optimizing your keywords for the US store and since it will most likely account for 85% of your book sales whereas the UK will only be about 10% or so.

AMAZON AUTHOR CENTRAL

It's not just the US and UK where Amazon has different international sites with different tags, likes, reviews and sales rankings. According to Amazon's most recent newsletter, they have separate Amazon Author Central platforms in the US, UK, Brazil, France and Germany.

Since very few of my sales personally come from Brazil, France or Germany, I don't worry too much about reviews, tags or likes on those sites. And if you're like me, a US-based author who writes only in English, I don't recommend you spend much time on it either. But for those of you who write in other languages or cater to international markets, make sure you apply the same principles taught in this book to your market and the unique Amazon website in the countries in which you wish to sell more Kindle books.

CHAPTER 9. WRITING MORE BOOKS, A GUARANTEED WAY TO SELL MORE KINDLE BOOKS!

One of the easiest ways to sell more Kindle books is to publish more books!

If you're a serious writer like me then I KNOW you have more than one great book in you. You probably have dozens, hundreds or even thousands of book ideas just waiting to be put into print (or Kindle).

After you've taken action on all the material in this book so far from adding the right keyword tags and categories of your book to writing a hot selling description, what should you do? Check your Kindle sales every hour and jump up and down when you make a new sale?

Well, certainly that's one way to do it but I think you'll find it to be a waste of time after a while and that the thrill pales in comparison to the accomplishment, achievement and payday you will receive from publishing your next book!

Marketing is so important for authors, especially independent Kindle publishers like you and me. But there's a fine line between marketing and busy work. Once you've found the right keyword tags and added them to your book, you're done with that! Don't re-hash it over and over, trying to find a better keyword. Just let it go – if you did the work right the first time you don't need to do it again!

One of the biggest traps I've seen other authors in The Society make is to become obsessed with having all the right tags and categories and checking sales on a daily or hourly basis. Oh, who am I kidding? I've done that too! And I can tell you from personal experience that it's a big waste of time and creative energy.

Once you've done the work you're done! Just let it be. Sure, you should check your sales at least once a month and check your rankings for different search terms in the Kindle Store to make sure your keywords and tags are positioning your book in the right places. But you only need to do that work once a month and it should only take an hour at most.

The rest of your working time as an author should be spent on creating new work! At the end of the day, your job as an author and creator is to create great books. Of course you want them to sell! That's why you are reading this book right now. But you have to be able to know when enough is enough and move on to your next book.

And I can tell you from personal experience that writing a new book can be the best thing to increase your book sales (once you've done all the marketing action steps mentioned so far). Having multiple books turns you into an established author rather than just a one-hit-wonder.

And it helps you build a platform. Would you rather learn from an author who's written 1 best-selling book or an author who's written 10 best-selling books? Obviously, you'd rather learn from the person who's done it over and over because the person who did it one time might just be a fluke!

Well, guess what! Your readers think the same way! The more books you have, the more books you will sell. Period. And not just because the new book will sell additional copies – but your older books will sell more copies as well! This is because it's very common for readers to buy multiple books from one author if they like your work.

To be totally honest with you, it's HIGHLY unlikely you will ever achieve the financial freedom and success you desire as an author with just one book. But if you write TEN books, it's HIGHLY likely that you will achieve all the goals you ever set for yourself as an author and then some!

Chapter 10. KDP Free Promotion Launch Formula

If you've never done a KDP free promotion before or if you have but didn't get the results you wanted, I'm going to share with you my personal free promotion launch formula that has always produced at least 638 downloads in 5 days (and as many as 22,257 for my nonfiction books).

Why Do A KDP Select Free Promotion?

So far, all of the strategies I've shared with you in this book are long-term sales strategies. They will produce a long-term increase in sales and may take 1-4 weeks to fully kick into effect (sometimes much faster, depending on how quickly Amazon makes updates to your book page).

But for brand new self-published authors with no platform or marketing experience, it can be very hard to "break into" the world of publishing and sell any significant amount of books. By offering your book for free for up to 5 days, you can get hundreds, thousands and even tens of thousands of downloads from readers.

This does several very important things:

1. Confidence

When you see thousands of people downloading and reading your book (even if it was free), it gives you the confidence to know that you've created something valuable and worthwhile.

You've got thousands of people who took their time to pick up your book and read it! For many first-time authors (myself included when I first started), this early success is crucial in cementing your confidence so that you will keep writing and promoting your books no matter what happens.

2. READERS!

If you have 10,000 downloads that means you have 10,000 new readers! They know your name and, if your book is good, they see you as an expert in your field. Of course, not everyone who downloads the free book will read it. Some might never even open it. But a good number WILL read your book. And it's 50 times easier to sell an existing reader one of your books than someone who doesn't know you at all.

If you have 10,000 free downloads, I guarantee you will have at least 100 readers who love your book and will be willing to share it with their friends and buy more of your books in the future. Every big following starts with a small group of interested people. And every loyal, raving fan reader you get will help you build the foundation of life-long success and financial freedom as an author.

3. INCREASED RANKINGS

If your book has never sold a single copy before your KDP Select promotion, I guarantee it will start selling after your free promotion. Amazon has separate sales rankings for paid books than for free books. This means the competition is much less for free books – and you're going to sell A LOT more because it's free.

If you choose your categories well as we talked about earlier and follow the marketing system you're about to see, you're pretty much guaranteed to become a #1 best-seller in your free category (often, my book will be the only free book in my category). This will get your book a lot of attention from browsers and will lead to new paid sales when your book's free promotion ends.

4. READER FEEDBACK

This is possibly the most important benefit of doing a free promotion for new authors – your readers will tell you how to improve your book! I've received reviews, emails and Facebook messages from readers and friends who read my book and told me about a typo I could fix or a question they had that wasn't clearly answered in the book. All of this feedback helps me improve my books – and it will help you too!

With a Kindle ebook, you can edit your book, re-upload it in 2 minutes and within 24 hours anyone who buys your book will get the new, edited version. So don't be afraid if you have a typo in your book – just publish it and you can fix it later! Perfectionism has killed the careers of many would-be best-selling authors.

Just make sure you do respond to feedback and improve your book if you can.

Now it's time to learn the Free Book Promotion Marketing System. Ready?

Choosing Your Free Days

The KDP Select program allows you to list your book for free on Amazon Kindle for up to 5 days. These 5 days can be all at once or in any combination of days you choose. For example, you could do a 5-day promotion all in a row or a 2-day and 3-day promotion, or 5 1-day promotions, etc… you get the point!

Because I write lots of books and I'm very busy with my other businesses, I choose to only do 5-day promotions and get it done with. This way, I can spend all of my marketing energy and resources for that 5-day time period and get the most results with the least effort.

However, if you only have one book and you REALLY want to get the most results out of your KDP free days, then I would recommend doing two promotions – one for 3 days and one for 2 days. The benefit of doing two promotions is that you will have twice the marketing efforts behind your book – you can do more social media promotions, press releases and use many more marketing strategies that we'll be covering in this chapter. Just realize you'll have to spend twice as much time promoting two free promotions.

For 5 Day Promotions

If you're going the simpler 5-day promotion route, then you want to start your promotion on a Saturday and run it through Wednesday. Why?

Because that's when most books are purchased on Kindle! According to a study from Digital Book Today, here are the

71

rankings for the most book sales per day on Amazon (the percentages are the percent of total sales for the week):

1. Monday 17.6%

2. Sunday 17.4%

3. Wednesday 13.8%

4. Thursday 13.5%

5. Tuesday 13.0%

6. Saturday 12.5%

7. Friday 12.2%

By Starting your promo on Saturday and ending on Wednesday, you're capturing 74.3% of the weekly sales potential in just 5 days – without any marketing (yet).

For those of you who want more data, you can read the whole article about the Kindle book sales study results here: http://bit.ly/U0JDiu

FOR 2-DAY / 3-DAY PROMOTIONS

For a 2-day promotion, start on Sunday and end on Monday.

For a 3-day promotion, start on Sunday and end on Tuesday.

PRE-LAUNCH STRATEGY

Okay you're ready to launch your book! The first step is to schedule your free promotion dates at least 3-4 weeks ahead of time. This will give you enough time to do all the pre-marketing to make your launch a huge success.

Press Releases

The first thing to do is write and schedule up to three press releases about your book's release and promotion. In The Society, we talk about writing press releases that "build on each other" meaning they start to tell a story and the story gets better and better in each release.

You can get a good basic, internet-only Press Release for $25 from Webwire.

For those on a tight budget, you can use Prlog.org for a free press release (with limited distribution).

You can get premium press releases from other sites for a few hundred dollars or so for even more exposure.

The first press release should announce your book's launch on Amazon exclusively, due to KDP select, and the date it will be available for sale (or mention that it's already available). The story for a non-fiction book is "Good news! There's a new book out that will help (insert type of people you help) get (insert what you help people get)." For a fiction book, the story is "Good news! There's a new book out that will whisk you away on a magical journey... (tell the story of your book)."

The second press release should announce your book's free promotion and the dates of the free promotion on Amazon. The story here is "Even better news! That new book that (repeat the story of the first release) is now FREE on these days."

The third press release should announce a special "bonus" or opportunity for people to learn more. You can do a Google+ Hangout, a webinar, teleseminar, or Q&A session with readers –

whatever you want. It's just a way to give even more value to buyers of your book and connect with your readers more. The story now is "Even better news WOW! Not only do you get this amazing book that (tell your story) but you also get it for free AND you get this really cool bonus (insert your bonus offer) that makes applying the information in the book that much easier." For fiction authors, you may have to be creative about the bonus. For example, you can create a high quality Desktop background wallpaper with characters from your book and give it to your readers during your promotion.

If you don't know how to write a press release, just search Google for press releases and copy their format. You can literally copy and paste the paragraphs and put in your info instead of theirs. Then you will know the format of your press release is professional. Then just proof read it and make sure it sounds how you want it to. No need to hire a PR expert!

COVER TESTING

As I talked about in the earlier chapter on picking a great Cover, the 3-4 weeks before your big launch are the perfect time to test out your new cover with Facebook ads. Make sure you test it before your promotion for maximum results (sales)!

Free Kindle Book Listings

Did you know there are hundreds of sites where you can list your free Kindle book promotions and they will give you FREE publicity and promote your book to avid Kindle readers?

Thanks to my friends in The Society who created this amazing list for all of us to use to promote our free Kindle Books.

List of Free Kindle Promotion Sites

Note: I know it's hard to copy and paste on a Kindle reader so you can copy/paste these links for listing you free Kindle books from my blog if you prefer here (also includes the 6 sites further on that you must list your book on the day your promotion starts): http://bit.ly/SwVMM3

1) Pixel of Ink http://www.pixelofink.com/sfkb

2) Ereader News Today

http://ereadernewstoday.com/ent-free-book-submissions

3) Bargain Ebook Hunter
http://bargainebookhunter.com/contact-us

4) That Book Place

http://www.thatbookplace.com/free-promo-submissions

5) Free Kindle Fiction http://freekindlefiction.blogspot.com
(Only for Fiction books)

6) Indie Book of the Day
http://indiebookoftheday.com/authors/free-on-kindle-listing

7) Free Book Dude

http://www.freebookdude.com/p/list-your-free-book.html

8) The-Cheap.net http://the-cheap.net/authors/free-promotion-opportunities/share-your-deal

9) Awesome Gang

http://awesomegang.com/submit-your-book

10) Free Kindle Books & Tips
http://www.fkbooksandtips.com/for-authors

10) FreeBookClub.org http://freebookclub.org

11) The Frugal Reader
http://thefrugalereader.wufoo.com/forms/frugal-freebie-submissions

12) Kindle Finds
http://kindlefinds.com/submissions/submission-form-kdp-free-day

13) Ebooksfreedaily
http://www.ebooksfreedaily.com/?page_id=16

14) Ebooklister http://ebooklister.net/submit.php

15) Centsibleereads

http://www.centsibleereads.com/p/for-authors.html

16) Freebookshub http://www.freebookshub.com/authors

17) Ebookshabit http://ebookshabit.com/for-authors

18) GoodKindles http://www.goodkindles.net

GoodKindles actually requires a $5+ donation to list your book but they will keep your listing up permanently unlike most sites and you can list there even if you're not doing a free promo.

How To List Your Books

Just click the links on the sites above and give them the information they need to post your book and promote it for you. Most often, you'll need the book title, link to the book on Amazon, ASIN (Amazon Sales Identification Number), a description, category and a few other items. It's pretty simple and should take less than 30 minutes to list a book on all 12 sites.

Make sure you list your book on all these sites AT LEAST 1 week in advance so that they have time to post it for you.

TWITTER MARKETING

Twitter is a great way to market your book during your free promotion and it's 100% free!

First of all, I recommend mentioning the following Tweeters who promote Kindle books and letting them know about your book with the link to it and the dates of your free promotion:

United States:

https://Twitter.com/#!/kindleEbooks

https://Twitter.com/#!/BookBub

https://Twitter.com/#!/KindleStuff

https://Twitter.com/#!/fkbt

https://Twitter.com/#!/DIGITALinktoday

https://Twitter.com/#!/freebookclub1

https://Twitter.com/#!/PixelofInk

https://Twitter.com/#!/FreeReadFeed

https://Twitter.com/#!/FreeKindleDude

https://twitter.com/free2kindle

https://twitter.com/freedailybooks

https://twitter.com/ZilchEbooks

https://twitter.com/KindleFreeBooks

https://twitter.com/FreeEbooksDaily

https://twitter.com/Kindle_FREE

United Kingdom:

Make sure to Tweet the link to your book on Amazon.co.uk to UK Tweeters – not your US link!

https://Twitter.com/#!/Free_UK_Ebooks

Most of these Twitter accounts will retweet your tweet to their followers and promote your book on Twitter during its free promotion.

Next, you can just tweet about the book yourself to your own Twitter followers and ask people to retweet and spread the message. You can use Hootsuite.com to schedule all your Tweets at once and get it done in 15 minutes or so.

On Your First Free Promo Day

Congratulations! It's the first day of your book promotion. The morning your book goes free, you've got several key marketing activities to do.

Free Site Listings

On day one of your free promotion, you can also post your book on the following sites (they only accept postings of books that are currently free so you can't do it ahead of time):

1) Snickslist.com snickslist.com/books/place-ad

2) Addicted To Ebooks addictedtoebooks.com/free

3) Daily Free Ebooks

daily-free-ebooks.com/suggest-free-ebook

4) Daily Cheap Reads dailycheapreads.com/category/free

5) Ereader IQ ereaderiq.com/contact

6) Best Ebooks World bestebooksworld.com/addlinks.asp

Facebook Marketing

If you have a Facebook profile or Fan Page, here's what I recommend you do to get the most exposure.

First, upload the image of the cover of your book to your Facebook profile and/or fan page. Then, post it with a description explaining your book is now free and anyone can download it, giving them the link to do so.

Here's an example of my free promotion post on Facebook – feel free to R&D (Rip-off and Duplicate!)

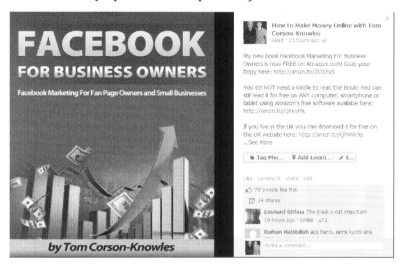

Here's the text I used to promote this book in the description of the picture:

"My new book Facebook Marketing For Business Owners is now FREE on Amazon.com! Grab your copy here: http://amzn.to/ZO5FsS

You do NOT need a Kindle to read the book! You can still read it for free on ANY computer, smartphone or tablet using Amazon's free software available here: http://amzn.to/QFexMk

If you live in the UK you can download it for free on the UK website here: http://amzn.to/QP4W9z

Facebook For Business Owners is the complete guide step-by-step for creating a Facebook Fan Page and turning it into a marketing machine for your business, attracting new leads on a daily basis.

If I can do it you can too!

Grab your free copy today (only available until Nov. 21st)."

Notice that in the description, I let people know they do NOT need a Kindle to read a Kindle book (which is a big misconception in the market, and since only 10% of people own Kindles, 90% of people won't buy unless you tell them they can read it without a Kindle!). I also give people the link to the free Kindle reader software to make it easier for them to buy and read the book. Always remember – the easier you make it to buy, the more people will buy!

PROMOTING YOUR POST

Facebook now has an option where you can Promote a post for both fan pages and personal profiles. When you click "Promote" underneath the post, you pay Facebook to show your post to more people. If you have a great cover image, this promoted post is likely to go viral and lead to hundreds if not thousands of new downloads for just a few dollars.

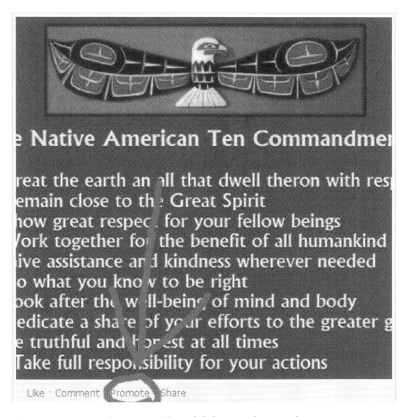

The Promote button should be right under your picture or status update post between the Comment and Share buttons.

OTHER MARKETING OPPORTUNITIES

There are millions of other ways you can promote your book during its free promotion period to maximize your downloads, new readers and ranking in the Kindle store. Out of everything I've tested, these strategies I mentioned above have been the most effective by far.

ACTION STEPS

If you're planning a free promo, plan it 3-4 weeks out at least so you have time to prepare for it. Then just re-read this chapter and follow the system step by step.

CHAPTER 11. WRITING PRODUCTIVITY TIPS, STRATEGIES AND RESOURCES

I first started writing "professionally" at age 7. My dad got a new computer and he bought a speed typing program that you could use on DOS. The program would give you typing challenges and then measure your typing speed. It also, thankfully, had trainings on how to become a faster typer. These I found invaluable and it's how I learned "proper" typing fundamentals, like where to place both hands and what keys to hit with which fingers.

Anyways, I used to spend HOURS a day on this speed typing program. I thought it was a game! And it was a LOT of fun for me. Well, my typing speed was over 80 wpm (words per minute) which I later found out was the speed that professionally trained typists often achieve. I honestly haven't tested myself since but I'm very tempted to as I write these words! My point, however, is that my fast typing speed and that speed typing program in particular have helped me immensely in my writing career.

I often hear other writers say they struggle to write fast enough. The only advice I can give you if that's the case is to go get yourself a speed typing program or a teacher who can mentor you in proper typing fundamentals and then practice (you'll have plenty of practice writing all those best-selling book ideas you have!).

After age 7 or 8, I got into a video game called Starcraft – I played it every day. And I would type to competitors and allies in the game. The thing with Starcraft is that it's a Real-Time

Strategy (RTS) game meaning that you have to constantly manage your buildings, workers, army and other things in the game. So you can't spend much time typing! I would venture to say my typing speed improved due to the competitiveness of the game and the necessity to spend as much time as possible playing and not typing.

At age 11, I remember writing a report on Winston Churchill for my 6th grade class project. I believe it was supposed to be just a few pages long. I read every book on Winston Churchill I could get my hands on, including a towering hardcover book that was over 700 pages long (and very dry, I might add). My paper was over 12 pages long, single-spaced, in type 12 font. My teacher was shocked at the length and clarity of the report and gave me an A+. I was happy with the grade but more thrilled with the act of writing itself – I thoroughly enjoyed writing that report!

At age 12 or 13, I started writing poetry on my computer in Word documents. I would just write whatever came to mind. Initially, it was for a school project but later it was just for fun, out of my own inspiration and curiosity. I thought nothing of it at the time and stopped writing poetry after a few months.

Shortly after, I met Mr. Gene Stowe, a journalist with an incredible ability to both write clearly and teach that skill to young students like myself at the time. He was my English teacher at the time and had rigorous writing standards. He taught me so much about writing and assigned numerous long writing assignments which gave me many hours of practice. Back then, I wasn't so happy about it but today I'm truly grateful for the writing experience I gained at such a young age.

At age 16, my English teacher gave the class an assignment to write a poem and submit it to a magazine or publication. I did and I was shocked to see it published in TeenInk magazine. My writing teacher even told me that I was very gifted and that I should write more poetry and seek to get it published. However, at the time I was very shy and modest and thought nothing of my prospects for a career in writing, poetry or any other kind. You would think it would have been obvious by now that I was destined to be a writer! But I had no idea and was much too timid to even consider it.

At age 19, as a freshman at Indiana University, I started to come out of my shell quite a bit. I started to write a book. I called it "Rich by 22" and even though I was 19 at the time, the book was meant to be both a decree to my own commitment to financial independence as well as a treatise on my personal philosophy of life and finances. I wrote several other manuscripts during my college years but never finished or even attempted to publish one of them.

I also started blogging at age 19 and had several blogs fail horribly in my early years as a blogger. Since then, I've started several successful blogs and continue to blog regularly (although I do outsource much of the writing on my blogs so that I can focus on my books for now).

Fast forward to February, 2012 (age 24). That's when someone told me I could publish a book on Amazon Kindle simply by uploading a Word document and it would be live in just a few hours. I couldn't believe it! Was it really that EASY to publish a book?

So I tried it. I had written an ebook with my mom, Dr. Candace Corson, that I was giving away on my blog to teach people about nutrition and living a healthy lifestyle. I decided to edit the book for Amazon and upload it. I was amazed at how people started buying it almost right away even without doing any promotion! I was hooked.

It inspired me to dust off my old manuscripts and books, finish them and publish them. I've now published 9 books in my own name and still have several of those books from my college years to complete. I've also published several books under pen names. And I've done it all with Amazon's amazing Kindle publishing platform. My only regret is that I wish I had taken action earlier when I first heard about Kindle years ago!

If you learn ANYTHING from my story, I hope you learn that it is NEVER too late to get started. Whether you've never even written a book, published a book or you've published dozens, you can always start over again. Kindle publishing makes it easy to get published and reach millions of people with your message. The only question is – what is your message? And are you willing to do what it takes to get it out there?

WRITING IN YOUR MIND

I often do my best writing in my mind while I'm sleeping, eating or doing something else. What do I mean by "writing in my mind?" Well, for me, it sounds like my inner voice reading words except they're words I've never heard or thought before – they're words for my book, a blog post, or some other purpose.

I find that these words flow through me like a Gift from God himself and if I don't capture these words and write them down or record them immediately, they could be lost forever. The truth is, I used to just let these words, thoughts and ideas slip by and forget them forever. Not anymore!

I've learned that these are often the most messages and ideas I have to share with the world anu ᴊᴜ ɪ ᴜᴀᴠᴄ created a system for ALWAYS recording anytime I start writing in my mind.

If I'm at home near my computer, I will stop whatever I'm doing (halfway through a meal or wake up in the middle of the night sometimes) and start typing those thoughts on my laptop. If that's not convenient, I will speak the words into a tape recorder. Nowadays I use my iPhone App QuickVoice Recorder as a recording device (it's a free app!).

As a last resort, I will take a notebook or scrap of paper and write down the main ideas, put them in my wallet or pocket and make sure to read them and write what flows as soon as I get back to writing on my laptop.

You never know when the inspiration for your next best-selling book will come from! Always be ready to write down or record your ideas. Just one good idea could change your life forever!

A WRITING EXERCISE

I've learned one writing exercise which I found very helpful in my early years as a blogger. I want to share it with you here in hopes that it will help you find your own unique voice as an author and be proud of who you are.

It's called the copycat writing exercise. Your task is to emulate your favorite writer and write two pages of your book as if you were them. For example, if you love Think and Grow

.ıch like I do, you would write two pages of your book as if you were Napoleon Hill writing it.

The idea of this exercise isn't to become a copycat but rather to learn about the VOICE of an author. Every person on this planet has a unique voice – and every great author lets their voice shine through their writing.

One of my favorite examples of this is T. Harv Eker and his book Secrets of the Millionaire Mind. When I first read that book at age 19, it made me laugh so hard! The book was incredibly inspirational and completely changed my "money blueprint" as Harv says. But it also made me laugh! It was unique, it was different. It didn't SOUND like any other book I'd ever read before (or since).

If you're trying to sound like a "professional author" or write as someone you're not, I highly recommend doing this copycat exercise because I think it will show you three very important things clearly:

First, every great author has a unique voice and it shows in their writing.

Second, you are NOT your favorite author (or any other author) and you do not need to sound like anyone but yourself.

Third, you DO have a unique voice to share with the world so stop trying to pretend you're someone else or something else. Just be yourself in your writing!

RECOMMENDED BOOKS ON WRITING

Two books have had a huge impact on my writing career. The first is *Simple and Direct* and the second is *On Writing Well*. Both these books are incredibly powerful tools in communicating through the written word and I can't recommend them highly enough for any author who wishes to make writing a career.

Another book I highly recommend is *The Science of Getting Rich* by Wallace D. Wattles. It was written over 100 years ago and is now in the public domain but I believe it has a powerful philosophy for living that will help anyone succeed in their field of endeavor, including writing.

ACTION STEPS

Decide now that you're going to make writing your career and become a professional. It doesn't matter if you're part-time, full-time or overtime! There is absolutely no shame in working in a 9-5 and being a part-time writer in your spare time. I believe the only real shame in life comes from not following your heart.

If your heart is telling you to be a writer then put your heart into your writing!

Always finish writing mid-sentence to make it easier to start writing again when you pick it back up.

Always write down or record your book ideas, inspirations, words, thoughts and ideas. Don't let these precious ideas slip away forever!

91

If you struggle with perfectionism, procrastination, writer's block or self-sabotage, then by all means start frictionless publishing. Publish your book on Kindle before "it's done" for 99 cents and then work your butt off to edit and polish it and make it the book it's meant to be.

BONUS INTERVIEWS WITH BEST-SELLING KINDLE AUTHORS

For this book I wanted to go beyond just being a book. I want it to be the most valuable resource you've ever had access to for kindle publishing and marketing ideas.

So I've hunted down some of the top Kindle authors on the planet and I'll be interviewing them over the coming weeks. All of these authors earn several thousand dollars a month in royalties from Kindle books and some earn far more.

But they won't be pitching you on their newest book, not even close. They will only be sharing their most precious marketing techniques, inspirational stories and ideas for new and budding authors like you who want to earn a full-time income as an author.

The first interview with Bev Flaxington, two-time bestselling and Gold-award winning author is now live and you can watch it for free here on YouTube: http://bit.ly/SrDcos

The second interview with Oli Hille, international bestselling author is live now as well. Watch it here on YouTube: http://bit.ly/ZtJFWN

SPECIAL FACEBOOK GROUP

Come join our Facebook group just for ethical authors like you who want to take their Kindle book sales to the next level. In this group we'll be sharing our successes, marketing tips and strategies with each other so that we can all continue to grow our businesses on Kindle.

It's also a great place to get any questions you have answered as well.

Come join us here on Facebook:
facebook.com/groups/KindlePublishers

FREE BLOGGING FOR BUSINESS TRAINING

Despite what other authors may say, blogging is a great way to make more money online. It's not necessarily a great way to sell more Kindle books, but I do sell several books a month from my blogs and once you've set it up, the sales keep coming automatically.

If you want to learn how to start a blog for your business that makes a profit, I've developed a free online training program to teach you everything from how to build your blog for free to getting traffic and monetizing it ethically.

You can get your blogging training at
BlogBusinessSchool.com

FREE TWITTER TRAINING

To thank you for buying this book I want to give you my best-selling book on How To Make Money With Twitter as a special bonus. I've been using Twitter for years to get hundreds of new leads a month for my online businesses and it's a great way to promote your books in very little time once you set the system up.

You can grab your free copy here: http://bit.ly/MlNne2

MOTIVATIONAL VIDEOS

I hope this book has been motivational for you and that it will inspire you to become a best-selling author and live the life of your dreams. That's what this information has done for me.

But I know you might not read this book every single day on your journey to becoming an even more successful author - so I'd like to share some inspiring videos with you to keep you motivated and moving forward in your career. You can watch them anytime you want to get motivated and stay motivated to make positive changes in your life.

I know these videos have helped me stay inspired, motivated and passionate – and I hope they help you too!

You might not like all of these videos – that's okay! Just watch the ones that resonate with you and make you feel good. If it works for you keep it. If it doesn't just throw it out!

LIST OF VIDEOS

Life Changing Motivational Video!! So Inspiring!

http://www.youtube.com/watch?v=Yxigy8HngvE

Best Motivational Video Scenes Ever Made! Inspiring

http://www.youtube.com/watch?v=KRXP-EKgMiw

The Greatest Inspirational Speech Ever Made by Charlie Chaplin (Motivation!)

http://www.youtube.com/watch?v=14pLwX107kE

97

The Motivational Speaker With No Arms and No Legs - Nick Vujicic

http://www.youtube.com/watch?v=YpaSZOq0C3U

How Bad Do You Want It? Success! Motivational Video Part 2

http://www.youtube.com/watch?v=0b1nCMIU2bM

Motivation! There Are No Limitations! Inspirational Video

http://www.youtube.com/watch?v=IQdi-TgCaxU

40 Inspirational and Motivational Speeches in 2 Minutes

http://www.youtube.com/watch?v=obJiTFKmNl4

Muhammad Ali Inspirational Speech (Cassius Clay Motivation)

http://www.youtube.com/watch?v=dGk0R63C0eM

I am a champion the greatest speech ever!

http://www.youtube.com/watch?v=fBZ-DLhISEE

Success: How Bad Do You Want It? Inspirational Video!

http://www.youtube.com/watch?v=IG1vac3TZ_Q

The Best Motivational Workout Video Ever!!

http://www.youtube.com/watch?v=49jD9AbITyg

Best Motivational Video For Startups And Entrepreneurs

http://www.youtube.com/watch?v=8NxDO6fA5rU

Winning Is A Habit! Best Motivational Video Ever!!

http://www.youtube.com/watch?v=U1hkzCK03tl

Truly The Best Motivational Video Ever! So Inspirational

http://www.youtube.com/watch?v=MLVHYIO6oso

The Best Motivational Video Ever - Don't Quit On Me Brock!!

http://www.youtube.com/watch?v=fOyiSEonUFA

A Note From The Author:

Thank you so much for taking the time to read this book. I'm excited for you to start your path to making the income of your dreams using Kindle ebook publishing.

If you have any questions of any kind, feel free to contact me directly at Tom@JuiceTom.com

You can follow me on Twitter: @JuiceTom

And connect with me on Facebok: Facebook.com/OnlineInternetMarketingHelp

You can check out my publishing blog for the latest updates here: TCKpublishing.com

I'm wishing you the best of health, happiness and success!

Here's to your success!

Tom Corson-Knowles

ABOUT THE AUTHOR

TOM CORSON-KNOWLES is the #1 Amazon bestselling author of *Facebook For Business Owners* and *How To Make Money With Twitter,* among others. He lives in Kapaa, Hawaii with his fiancé. Tom loves educating and inspiring other authors and entrepreneurs to succeed and live the life of their dreams.

Learn more about Tom at Amazon.com/author/business

OTHER BOOKS BY TOM CORSON-KNOWLES

The Kindle Writing Bible

The Amazon Analytics Bible

How To Make Money With Twitter

Ninja Book Marketing Secrets

The Blog Business Book

The Kindle Formatting Bible

101 Ways To Start A Business For Less Than $1,000

Facebook For Business Owners

Rich by 22: How To Achieve Business Success at an Early Age

How To Reduce Your Debt Overnight

The Network Marketing Manual

Dr. Corson's Top 5 Nutrition Tips

The Vertical Gardening Guidebook

One Last Thing...

Please leave a review for this book on Amazon! Whether you loved it or hated it, your feedback will help us make it even better for future readers.

You can review it here on Amazon: http://amzn.to/Q3pxWa

Thank you so much!

Printed in Great Britain
by Amazon